A Brief History of Montana

KJ Smith

Copyright © 2025 KJ Smith

All rights reserved.

ISBN: 9798306616520

Contents

INTRODUCTION 1
THE LAND & ITS FIRST PEOPLES 5
EXPLORATION & EARLY CONTACTS..9
THE GOLD RUSH ERA & SETTLEMENT 14
THE NATIVE AMERICAN STRUGGLE FOR LAND 19
STATEHOOD & EARLY GOVERNMENT..26
RANCHING & AGRICULTURE 34
INDUSTRIALIZATION & RESOURCE EXTRACTION 42
THE CONSERVATION MOVEMENT 51
THE GREAT DERESSION & WWII 60
POST-WAR GROWTH & MODERNIZATION 69
CONTEMPORARY ERA...79
CONCLUSION 89
ABOUT THE AUTHOR 92

INTRODUCTION

Montana, known as "The Treasure State," is a place where history, nature, and culture converge in a rugged landscape of vast plains, towering mountains, and pristine wilderness. Defined by a spirit of independence and a connection to the land, Montana's history is as dramatic and diverse as its scenery. From the ancient tribal cultures who first called this place home to the gold rushers, fur trappers, and homesteaders who transformed its valleys and rivers, Montana's story is one of resilience, resourcefulness, and often, survival.

Nestled in the Northern Rockies, Montana is a place where the whispers of the past echo through sprawling prairies and shadowed canyons. Its story is not just one of American settlement but a testament to the deep-rooted cultures of Native American tribes who cultivated lives here long before European explorers arrived. Tribes like the Blackfeet, Crow, Salish, Kootenai, and many others had built their lives around the land, developing sophisticated social structures and spiritual practices intricately connected to Montana's mountains, rivers, and plains. For them, this land was not a frontier but a well-worn home, rich with meaning and history. They hunted, fished, and thrived here, creating enduring traditions and legacies that would later be challenged and transformed by outside forces.

In the early 19th century, the Lewis and Clark Expedition marked the beginning of a new chapter for Montana, introducing the territory to the broader world. Their journey opened the door to a wave of fur traders, explorers, and prospectors who saw potential riches in Montana's forests, rivers, and mountains. Over time, the quest for gold and resources brought a flood of settlers, altering the land's ancient rhythms and reshaping its identity. As they built towns, dug mines, and established ranches, they set in motion a series of changes that would forever alter Montana's landscape and culture.

Yet Montana's story is not simply one of transformation and expansion. It is also a story of resistance and resilience. Native tribes fought to protect their territories, their traditions, and their way of life. Their resistance, as well as the conflicts over land and resources, marked an era of violence, displacement, and heartache that reverberates through Montana's history. The Battle of the Little Bighorn, known as Custer's Last Stand, stands as a powerful symbol of this turbulent era—a moment when cultures clashed and the future of Montana hung in the balance.

Montana's identity was further shaped by its pursuit of statehood, achieved in 1889, which brought new challenges and opportunities. In the years that followed, mining and ranching became the backbone of the state's economy, while railroads and telegraph lines connected its towns and cities to the rest of the country. But these industries came with a cost, leaving environmental scars that would later prompt the rise of a passionate conservation movement. The establishment of Glacier National Park in 1910 and other preservation efforts underscored a growing awareness of Montana's ecological significance and the importance of protecting its natural heritage.

Throughout the 20th century, Montana continued to evolve, adapting to new economic realities and shifting demographics. The decline of the mining industry in the post-war era gave rise to tourism as people from around the world came to experience the grandeur of places like Yellowstone and Glacier. This new era brought a renewed appreciation for the state's vast landscapes and open spaces, adding to Montana's appeal as a destination where nature and solitude reign supreme.

Today, Montana stands at a crossroads, its future shaped by both tradition and innovation. The state's economy, once rooted in agriculture, mining, and timber, now includes diverse industries like technology, tourism, and outdoor recreation. Yet, Montana remains a place where the past is ever-present, where the wildness of the land is both a source of beauty and a reminder of the state's unique legacy. Its people continue to grapple with issues of land use, Indigenous rights, environmental preservation, and economic sustainability, each shaped by the intricate tapestry of Montana's past.

In this book, we'll journey through the story of Montana—from the ancient traditions of its first peoples to the fur trade, the homesteading era, and the industrial boom of mining. We'll explore how its wild landscapes became symbols of American wilderness and how a deep-rooted spirit of independence has shaped Montana's identity and values. As we trace this history, we'll see how Montana's past influences its present, illuminating a story that is at once uniquely American and profoundly Montanan.

So, welcome to Montana—a place where history is as sweeping as the Big Sky itself, where the legacies of those who came before live on in its rivers, forests, and plains. Whether you are drawn by the rugged charm of its landscape or the rich stories of its past, Montana's history promises a journey that is as expansive and unforgettable as the land it calls home.

THE LAND & ITS FIRST PEOPLES

Montana is a land of breathtaking contrasts, where rugged mountains rise dramatically from the plains, and clear rivers carve their way through deep canyons. This vast and varied landscape has been shaped by millennia of geological activity, from ancient volcanic eruptions to the slow erosion of glaciers, resulting in a region rich in natural resources and beauty. But long before European settlers arrived, this land was home to Indigenous peoples who had formed deep connections with its diverse environments, developing cultures and lifestyles uniquely suited to their surroundings.

The history of Montana is deeply intertwined with that of its first peoples, the Native American tribes who have inhabited the region for thousands of years. Archaeological evidence suggests that humans have lived in what is now Montana for over 12,000 years, with a complex tapestry of societies emerging over time. The vast expanse of Montana provided a wealth of resources, from the bison that roamed the plains to the salmon-rich rivers of the west, enabling Indigenous tribes to thrive in this diverse environment.

Among the most prominent tribes in Montana were the Blackfeet, Crow, Salish, Kootenai, and Assiniboine. Each tribe had its own distinct culture, language, and social structure, yet they shared a common reverence for the land and its bounty. The Blackfeet, for instance, roamed the northern plains and relied heavily on bison for sustenance, clothing, and shelter. Their nomadic lifestyle was guided by the seasonal migrations of the herds, and they developed a rich cultural heritage filled with stories, traditions, and ceremonies honoring the animals that sustained them.

The Crow people, known for their vibrant artwork and intricate beadwork, inhabited the region around the Yellowstone River. They practiced both agriculture and hunting, cultivating crops such as corn, beans, and squash while also relying on bison and deer for meat. The Crow's social structure was matrilineal, with clan membership and inheritance passed through the female line, creating a society that valued the roles of women as leaders and caretakers.

In contrast, the Salish and Kootenai tribes, located in the mountainous western regions of Montana, had a different relationship with the land. They were skilled fishers and gatherers, relying on the abundant rivers for salmon and the forests for roots, berries, and game. Their cultures were steeped in spirituality, with a deep respect for the natural world and the belief that all living things were interconnected.

The arrival of Europeans in the early 19th century marked a turning point in the lives of Montana's Indigenous peoples. The Lewis and Clark Expedition, which passed through the region in 1805, opened the door for further exploration and settlement. Their journals detailed encounters with Native tribes, describing both the beauty of the land and the complex societies they encountered. However, this newfound interest in Montana would soon lead to significant disruptions for its Indigenous inhabitants.

As fur traders and settlers began to arrive, the balance of life for Native tribes was irrevocably altered. The fur trade brought new goods and technologies, but it also introduced diseases that decimated populations who had no immunity to such illnesses. The bison, central to the livelihoods of many tribes, were hunted to near extinction by both settlers and commercial hunters, leading to economic and cultural upheaval. The treaties signed between tribes and the U.S. government often favored the interests of settlers, resulting in the loss of traditional lands and hunting grounds.

Despite these challenges, Montana's Indigenous peoples have demonstrated remarkable resilience. Many tribes worked to adapt to the changing circumstances, finding ways to navigate the complexities of a rapidly evolving world while striving to preserve their cultural heritage. Efforts to revitalize languages, traditions, and community connections are evident today as tribes seek to reclaim their identities and assert their rights in the modern era.

Understanding the rich history of Montana's first peoples is crucial to comprehending the broader narrative of the state. Their stories, traditions, and ongoing struggles for recognition and sovereignty highlight the profound connection between the land and its inhabitants. As we delve deeper into Montana's history, we will continue to encounter the echoes of these vibrant cultures, reminding us that the past is not merely a series of events but a living tapestry that shapes the present and future of this remarkable region.

In the chapters that follow, we will explore the tumultuous journey of Montana—from the early encounters between Native tribes and European explorers to the transformative events that shaped its identity as a state. Through this exploration, we will honor the enduring legacies of Montana's Indigenous peoples and reflect on the complex interplay of culture, conflict, and adaptation that defines this beautiful land.

EXPLORATION & EARLY CONTACTS

The vastness of Montana's landscape has long captured the imagination of explorers, adventurers, and settlers. Its mountains, rivers, and plains were not merely geographical features but realms of potential and discovery. In the late 18th and early 19th centuries, the region drew the attention of explorers who sought to chart its uncharted territories and uncover the wealth of resources hidden within. This chapter delves into the era of exploration, focusing on the significant figures and events that marked the beginning of Montana's transformation from a land inhabited by Indigenous peoples to one that would soon see waves of settlers and newcomers.

The Age of Exploration

As European powers expanded their reach across the continent, the vast expanse of Montana remained largely unknown. The Spanish, French, and British had all shown interest in the region, but it wasn't until the early 1800s that significant exploration efforts began. The quest for knowledge and resources fueled the ambitions of several notable explorers.

One of the most famous expeditions to traverse the area was the Lewis and Clark Expedition (1804–1806). Commissioned by President Thomas Jefferson, the journey aimed to explore the newly acquired Louisiana Territory and find a practical route to the Pacific Ocean. Meriwether Lewis and William Clark, along with their party of skilled frontiersmen, navigated treacherous rivers and rugged terrain, encountering diverse landscapes and peoples along the way.

In their journey, Lewis and Clark reached the confluence of the Missouri and Yellowstone Rivers, a critical juncture that would later play a significant role in Montana's settlement. Their journals provide valuable insights into the land, its resources, and the Native tribes they encountered, including the Mandan and Hidatsa, who lived along the riverbanks. The expedition recorded descriptions of the natural beauty of the region, highlighting its potential for agriculture, trade, and settlement.

However, the encounters with Native American tribes were often fraught with complexity. The explorers' interactions ranged from friendly exchanges to tense confrontations, reflecting the broader dynamics of cultural exchange and conflict that would characterize future relations. The expedition also marked the beginning of a new era, one that would see the encroachment of settlers on Native lands and the profound transformations that followed.

The Fur Trade

The early 1800s also saw the emergence of the fur trade as a driving force in the region's economy. As the demand for beaver pelts soared in Europe and the Eastern United States, fur traders began to venture into Montana in search of riches. Companies like the American Fur Company, founded by John Jacob Astor, established trading posts throughout the region, significantly impacting both the economy and the culture of the Indigenous peoples.

Trappers and traders often formed alliances with Native tribes, relying on their knowledge of the land and resources. This exchange was mutually beneficial; Indigenous peoples gained access to European goods such as firearms, metal tools, and textiles, while traders obtained valuable furs. However, this relationship also brought unintended consequences. The introduction of new diseases, to which Native peoples had no immunity, led to devastating population declines among tribes already struggling with the pressures of encroaching settlers.

The fur trade period also witnessed the establishment of prominent trading posts, such as Fort Benton, which became a hub for trade along the Missouri River. These posts facilitated the movement of goods and people, serving as gateways for settlers who would soon follow the trails blazed by traders and explorers.

The Influence of the Catholic Missionaries

As exploration and trade expanded, so too did the presence of European missionaries. The Jesuits and other religious orders arrived in Montana with the intention of converting Indigenous peoples to Christianity. Their missions played a dual role: they sought to spread their faith while also documenting the languages, customs, and traditions of the tribes they encountered.

Missionaries established missions across the region, including the St. Ignatius Mission founded by the Jesuits among the Salish people. These missions became centers of education and agriculture, introducing European farming techniques to Native communities. While some Indigenous peoples embraced these new practices, others resisted, seeing the encroachment of missionaries as another threat to their way of life.

The missionaries' interactions with Native tribes were complex; while they sought to provide education and health care, their presence often symbolized a broader cultural invasion. The tension between the desire to preserve traditional beliefs and the push for conversion would shape the future of Indigenous communities in Montana.

The Path to Settlement

The exploration and early contacts of the late 18th and early 19th centuries set the stage for significant changes in Montana. The region, once a largely untouched wilderness, began to transform as settlers, drawn by the promise of land and opportunity, ventured into the area. The Lewis and Clark Expedition's findings fueled curiosity and interest in Montana's potential, and soon thereafter, waves of homesteaders would arrive, eager to stake their claims.

The allure of gold would soon further accelerate this process. The discovery of gold in the neighboring territories ignited a rush of prospectors and settlers seeking fortune and adventure. Montana's vast resources would soon draw people from across the nation, heralding an era of rapid settlement and transformation that would forever alter the landscape and the lives of its inhabitants.

As we progress through Montana's history, it is essential to recognize the profound impacts of these early explorations and interactions. They laid the groundwork for the complexities of relationships between Indigenous peoples and settlers, a dynamic that would shape the state's identity for generations to come. The stories of exploration, trade, and the cultural exchange that unfolded during this period remind us that Montana's history is a tapestry woven from diverse threads—each contributing to the rich and multifaceted narrative of this remarkable state.

THE GOLD RUSH ERA & SETTLEMENT

The discovery of gold in the mid-19th century marked a pivotal turning point in Montana's history, transforming the region from a largely uncharted wilderness into a bustling center of prospecting, settlement, and conflict. The allure of gold not only drew thousands of fortune seekers to the area but also set in motion a series of events that would profoundly impact both the landscape and the lives of its Indigenous peoples. This chapter explores the gold rush era in Montana, highlighting the rush for riches, the development of mining towns, and the resulting social and economic changes that reshaped the state.

The Discovery of Gold

The first significant gold discovery in Montana occurred in 1862 along the banks of Grasshopper Creek in what is now Beaverhead County. Miners from the nearby gold rushes in California and Colorado were drawn to the news, sparking a flood of prospectors into the region. The initial discovery was made by a group of miners led by John White, who stumbled upon the precious metal while working in the area. News of the strike spread quickly, igniting what would become one of the most significant gold rushes in American history.

As prospectors flocked to Montana, they established mining camps that would soon develop into bustling towns. Virginia City, founded in 1863, became the first major mining town and a key center of the gold rush. It was a rough-and-tumble place, filled with miners, merchants, and opportunists looking to make their fortunes. Virginia City's population swelled to nearly 10,000 people at its peak, with saloons, boarding houses, and shops catering to the influx of prospectors.

The discovery of gold brought not only miners but also entrepreneurs eager to capitalize on the burgeoning economy. Businessmen established supply stores, equipment manufacturers, and services catering to the needs of the mining community. The impact of this economic boom was profound, as it created jobs, stimulated commerce, and attracted people from diverse backgrounds, including immigrants from Europe, African Americans, and Chinese laborers.

The Mining Boom

The mining boom spread throughout Montana, with new discoveries being made in areas such as Alder Gulch, Last Chance Gulch (in present-day Helena), and the Black Hills. Each new strike prompted further waves of migration, with thousands of hopeful miners pouring into the territory. However, the gold rush was not without its challenges. The rush for riches often led to violent conflicts, as competition for claims escalated and tensions mounted between rival miners.

In many cases, miners formed vigilante committees to maintain order in the lawless camps. These groups often took justice into their own hands, establishing a code of conduct and enforcing it with little regard for due process. While these vigilante systems provided some measure of order, they also highlighted the chaotic and often dangerous nature of life in the mining towns.

Despite the hardships, the gold rush era was marked by innovation and determination. Miners developed new techniques for extracting gold, including hydraulic mining and the use of stamps to crush ore. The influx of capital from successful mines led to infrastructure development, including roads, railways, and telegraph lines that connected remote mining camps to the outside world. This burgeoning infrastructure laid the foundation for future economic growth in Montana.

The Impact on Native Americans

As settlers flooded into Montana in search of gold, the consequences for Indigenous peoples were severe. The encroachment of miners and settlers disrupted traditional lands, hunting grounds, and ways of life. Tribes were increasingly forced into conflict as they defended their territories against the influx of settlers. The disruption of bison herds due to overhunting and habitat loss also had devastating effects on tribes that relied on these animals for sustenance.

The U.S. government, eager to promote settlement and economic development in Montana, pursued policies that marginalized Native communities. Treaties were often negotiated under duress, leading to the cession of vast tracts of land that had been inhabited by Indigenous peoples for centuries. The signing of treaties such as the Fort Laramie Treaty of 1868 resulted in the establishment of reservations, which confined tribes to specific areas, further eroding their traditional ways of life.

Conflicts escalated as tensions between settlers and Indigenous tribes reached a boiling point. The conflicts culminated in several violent encounters, including the infamous Battle of the Little Bighorn in 1876, where a coalition of Native American tribes, including the Lakota and Cheyenne, decisively defeated General George Armstrong Custer and his forces. Although this battle was a moment of triumph for the tribes, it ultimately led to intensified military campaigns against them and the further loss of land and autonomy.

The Transition to Statehood

The gold rush era laid the groundwork for Montana's eventual statehood. As mining continued to thrive, the territory's population surged, attracting settlers who sought not only wealth but also a new life in the West. Towns like Helena, Butte, and Anaconda emerged as key players in the mining industry, leading to a diverse economy that extended beyond gold mining into agriculture, timber, and livestock.

By 1889, Montana had grown sufficiently in population and infrastructure to apply for statehood. The transition to statehood marked a new chapter in Montana's history, formalizing its place in the Union and setting the stage for the challenges and opportunities that lay ahead.

As we reflect on the gold rush era, it becomes clear that this period was defined not just by the search for wealth but also by the complex interplay of cultures, ambitions, and conflicts. The gold rush forever altered Montana's landscape, economy, and society, shaping the identities of its inhabitants and the legacy of its Indigenous peoples. The echoes of this transformative period continue to resonate, reminding us of the challenges and triumphs that defined Montana's path to becoming a state.

THE NATIVE AMERICAN STRUGGLE FOR LAND

As waves of settlers, gold prospectors, and homesteaders flooded into Montana during the 19th century, the Indigenous peoples of the region faced immense challenges. The arrival of these newcomers brought profound disruptions to their way of life, forcing Native tribes to defend their territories, adapt to foreign pressures, and grapple with broken promises and ever-changing policies. This chapter delves into the struggle for land that marked the latter half of the 19th century, exploring the battles, treaties, and complex relationship between Native Americans and the U.S. government.

The Conflict Begins: Encroachment and Displacement

Before the arrival of settlers, Montana was a land where numerous Native American tribes lived in relative harmony with the landscape, adapting their lifestyles to the natural rhythms of the region. The Blackfeet, Crow, Sioux, Cheyenne, and Salish, among others, hunted, fished, and traveled according to the seasonal availability of resources. However, as news of Montana's fertile land and mineral wealth spread, the territory increasingly became a destination for settlers and fortune-seekers, which put enormous pressure on Native communities.

The discovery of gold in the early 1860s triggered a flood of miners into territories that had long been recognized as Native lands. Suddenly, areas that had been hunting grounds for generations were overrun by settlers hoping to strike it rich. The bison, a cornerstone of many tribes' cultures and a primary food source, were hunted relentlessly, leading to their near extinction. This depletion devastated the traditional economies of tribes like the Blackfeet, Crow, and Lakota, who depended on bison for food, shelter, and clothing.

The influx of settlers was accompanied by an escalation in tensions between Native peoples and newcomers. These tensions often boiled over into violence, with settlers encroaching on tribal lands and Native warriors retaliating to protect their families and homes. The U.S. government, meanwhile, increasingly took the side of the settlers, pushing forward with a series of policies aimed at pacifying and relocating Native tribes, often disregarding earlier promises or agreements.

The Treaty Era and Broken Promises

In an attempt to mitigate the growing conflict between Native tribes and settlers, the U.S. government entered into a series of treaties with Montana's Native peoples. These treaties were intended to clearly delineate Native territories and guarantee rights to specific lands. However, the promises made in these agreements were rarely kept, and the treaties themselves often represented only a temporary lull in the conflict.

The Fort Laramie Treaty of 1851 and its subsequent revision in 1868 were among the most significant treaties impacting Montana's Native peoples. The initial treaty sought to establish peace by assigning distinct territories to different tribes, including the Crow, Blackfeet, and Sioux. However, as more settlers moved westward, new demands for land arose, leading to repeated infringements on these designated territories. The revised 1868 treaty was meant to guarantee the Sioux and Cheyenne exclusive use of the Powder River Country, but ongoing gold discoveries and pressure from settlers led to a series of violations by the government and white settlers alike.

For the Crow people, treaties meant shrinking territory and the loss of key hunting grounds. Originally occupying vast stretches of land, the Crow saw their landbase continually reduced by treaties that carved out portions for white settlers and new railroad routes. The Crow had allied themselves with the U.S. government in hopes of securing protection from the encroaching Sioux, but they found that even alliances with the government did little to protect their lands from being whittled away.

The Great Sioux War and the Battle of the Little Bighorn

The growing tensions between the U.S. government and Native tribes culminated in the Great Sioux War of 1876–1877, one of the most well-known conflicts in American history. Among the pivotal events of this conflict was the Battle of the Little Bighorn, fought in June 1876. This battle became known as "Custer's Last Stand" and was one of the rare victories for Native Americans during the Indian Wars.

Led by prominent leaders like Sitting Bull, Crazy Horse, and Gall, the Sioux and Cheyenne warriors united to resist the encroachment of the U.S. Army. In one of the most famous confrontations, the combined Native forces decisively defeated General George Armstrong Custer and his 7th Cavalry at the Little Bighorn River. The battle, while a significant triumph for Native forces, had a tragic irony: it only led to more aggressive military campaigns by the U.S. government. The overwhelming response in the aftermath of Little Bighorn ultimately led to further defeats and the forced relocation of the Sioux and Cheyenne to reservations.

The victory at Little Bighorn was a moment of unity and hope for Native peoples, but it also underscored the desperation of their situation. The federal government responded by doubling down on efforts to suppress Indigenous resistance and by sending in even more troops to force Native peoples onto reservations, stripping them of their ability to hunt freely and live independently.

Life on Reservations

Following the Indian Wars of the late 19th century, many of Montana's Native tribes were forced onto reservations, which often comprised only a fraction of their traditional territories. Life on the reservations was difficult and marked by poverty, disease, and a lack of opportunities. Promises of food, supplies, and education made by the U.S. government were often unfulfilled, and tribes found themselves reliant on the federal government for survival. Traditional ways of life that had been passed down for generations were severely disrupted, and efforts by the government to "civilize" Native peoples further eroded cultural practices and social structures.

The Dawes Act of 1887, also known as the General Allotment Act, dealt another blow to Montana's tribes. Under the pretense of promoting self-sufficiency, the Dawes Act subdivided reservation land into individual allotments, intending to assimilate Native peoples into the agrarian lifestyle of white settlers. However, the outcome was often disastrous. Land that was not allotted to individual Native families was declared "surplus" and sold to non-Native settlers. This act led to the further loss of communal land and left tribes with fragmented land holdings, unsuitable for sustaining their communities.

Resilience and Cultural Preservation

Despite the enormous hardships imposed by U.S. government policies and the relentless pressure of settlers, Montana's Native American tribes demonstrated remarkable resilience. They found ways to adapt to their new realities while striving to keep their cultural traditions alive. Leaders like Chief Plenty Coups of the Crow Nation worked tirelessly to navigate relations with the U.S. government in ways that preserved their people's dignity and way of life. Plenty Coups, for example, advocated for education and skill development that would allow his people to adapt to the changing world while maintaining a sense of cultural pride.

The early 20th century saw a growing movement among Native tribes to preserve their languages, ceremonies, and traditions, even in the face of relentless efforts to force assimilation. Tribal elders worked to pass down traditional knowledge through storytelling, teaching younger generations about the values and practices that had sustained their people for centuries.

In the 1930s, the Indian Reorganization Act provided a measure of relief, allowing tribes more control over their internal governance and a degree of self-determination. This marked a turning point in the relationship between Native tribes and the U.S. government, as tribes began to regain a voice in managing their own affairs and reclaiming aspects of their culture and identity.

The Native American struggle for land in Montana was marked by resilience in the face of overwhelming challenges. The story of this struggle is one of endurance, courage, and a determination to preserve a way of life that was deeply connected to the land. While the treaties, battles, and policies of the 19th century significantly altered the lives of Montana's Indigenous peoples, they also left behind a legacy of resistance and survival.

As we move forward in Montana's history, we will see how the impacts of this era continued to reverberate, shaping the political, social, and cultural fabric of the state. The struggle for land was not just a fight for territory; it was a battle for the right to maintain an identity, a heritage, and a deep connection to the land that has always been at the heart of Montana's story.

STATEHOOD & EARLY GOVERNMENT

The late 19th century was a transformative time for Montana. Following decades of exploration, settlement, and conflict, Montana's journey toward statehood culminated in its official admission to the Union in 1889. The path to statehood was far from straightforward; it was marked by political maneuvering, economic changes, and a desire to formalize Montana's growing significance in the national landscape. This chapter explores the events that led to Montana becoming the 41st state, the establishment of its early government, and the challenges faced by its citizens as they sought to build a functioning society amidst the changing tides of the American West.

The Push for Statehood

By the 1880s, Montana's population was steadily increasing due to several factors: the discovery of mineral wealth, expanding ranching opportunities, and the extension of the Northern Pacific Railroad into the region. The railroads connected Montana to the rest of the nation, enabling not only easier transportation but also an influx of settlers, goods, and ideas. Mining, ranching, and agriculture provided economic stability and fueled dreams of prosperity, contributing to the momentum for statehood.

The increasing population and economic growth created a demand for more local control and autonomy. As a U.S. territory, Montana was governed by officials appointed by the federal government, leaving residents with limited say in their governance. Territorial leaders and influential businessmen began to advocate for statehood, viewing it as a means of gaining greater political representation and securing Montana's future as a prominent part of the United States.

The federal government, meanwhile, was open to the idea of admitting new states, particularly in the West, to solidify American claims over territories and support the push for expansion. In 1889, the Enabling Act was passed by Congress, granting Montana and several other territories the opportunity to draft constitutions and apply for admission to the Union. Montana's leaders moved swiftly, calling for a constitutional convention to lay the groundwork for statehood.

The Constitutional Convention

In July 1889, Montana's constitutional convention convened in Helena, the territorial capital. Delegates from across the territory gathered to draft a constitution that would establish the framework of governance for the future state. The convention was a lively gathering, with a range of voices representing Montana's diverse population—ranchers, miners, merchants, lawyers, and politicians, each with their own ideas of how the state should be governed.

The constitution they drafted reflected Montana's frontier spirit, balancing the interests of various economic groups and providing for a state government that would promote growth while protecting individual freedoms. Among the key provisions was the creation of a bicameral legislature, composed of a Senate and a House of Representatives, mirroring the federal model. The constitution also established an executive branch, headed by a governor, as well as a judicial system to oversee the interpretation and enforcement of laws.

Montana's constitution made provisions for the regulation of industries critical to the state's economy, such as mining and ranching, while also establishing public education as a priority. The delegates recognized the importance of education in shaping Montana's future and provided for the establishment of schools, ensuring that the state's children would have access to the resources needed to succeed.

In addition to addressing governance and education, the constitution reflected the concerns of the people regarding civil liberties and individual rights. The delegates ensured that Montana's citizens would be guaranteed basic freedoms, including the right to free speech, assembly, and religious practice. These provisions were crucial to the residents of a state whose population was marked by diversity and a strong sense of individualism.

Admission to the Union

On November 8, 1889, President Benjamin Harrison signed the proclamation admitting Montana as the 41st state of the United States. The news was met with celebration across the state, as residents rejoiced at the prospect of greater self-determination and a more prominent place within the nation. Statehood represented an opportunity for Montana to fully participate in the democratic process, with the ability to elect representatives to Congress and have a voice in national affairs.

The admission of Montana to the Union was also significant for the region's economic growth. Statehood attracted new investments, and the development of infrastructure accelerated, with railroads continuing to expand, connecting more of Montana's towns and cities. The formal recognition of Montana as a state lent legitimacy to its institutions, encouraging further migration and development.

However, the transition to statehood was not without its challenges. The newly established state government faced the task of managing the diverse and sometimes conflicting interests of its citizens. The booming mining industry, dominated by powerful companies like the Anaconda Copper Mining Company, often found itself at odds with the ranching and agricultural sectors. Balancing the interests of these key industries while ensuring the well-being of the state's citizens would prove to be a complex undertaking for Montana's leaders.

Early Political Dynamics

Montana's early political landscape was shaped by fierce competition between the Democratic and Republican parties. The two parties vied for control of the state government, each representing different constituencies and economic interests. The Democratic Party found support among the mining communities and laborers, while the Republican Party was backed by many of the state's ranchers, businessmen, and settlers from more urban areas.

The influence of powerful mining companies, particularly the Anaconda Company, played a significant role in shaping Montana's early politics. The company's influence over the state's economy translated into considerable political power, with company officials often wielding influence over elections and legislation. This period, known as the "Copper

Collar" era, was marked by accusations of corruption and corporate control, with critics arguing that the interests of ordinary Montanans were often subordinated to those of powerful industrialists.

Labor movements also began to gain momentum during this period, as miners and other workers sought to improve their working conditions and wages. The labor struggles that emerged in Montana were part of a broader national movement, with unions forming to advocate for workers' rights. The mining industry, in particular, was fraught with dangers, and workers demanded better safety measures and fair compensation for the risks they faced. The formation of the Butte Miners' Union in 1878 marked the beginning of organized labor in the state, setting the stage for future conflicts and negotiations between labor and industry.

Infrastructure and Education

With statehood came a renewed focus on building the infrastructure necessary for Montana's growth. Roads, railways, and bridges were constructed to connect the state's towns and cities, facilitating the movement of people and goods. The expansion of the railroad network was particularly significant, allowing Montana's agricultural products, minerals, and other resources to reach national and international markets.

The state also invested in education, fulfilling the promise made during the constitutional convention. Schools were established in towns and cities across Montana, and in 1893, the Montana State University was founded in Bozeman, providing higher education opportunities to the state's residents. The establishment of public schools and universities reflected a commitment to preparing the next generation for the challenges and opportunities of life in Montana.

The Challenges of Statehood

While statehood brought opportunities, it also brought challenges. Montana's economy remained heavily dependent on resource extraction, particularly mining, which was subject to boom-and-bust cycles. The state's prosperity was often tied to fluctuations in the prices of copper, gold, and silver, leading to periods of economic instability. The need to diversify the economy and create a more stable foundation for growth became a central issue for Montana's leaders in the years following statehood.

Additionally, the relationship between the state government and Montana's Native American tribes remained fraught with tension. Despite the promises made in treaties, the federal and state governments continued to push for the assimilation of Native peoples, often through policies that undermined traditional ways of life. The Dawes Act, which sought to allot reservation land to individual Native families, further eroded tribal sovereignty and led to the loss of significant amounts of Native land. The struggle for Native rights and recognition would continue to be a critical issue in Montana's history.

Conclusion

The journey to statehood was a defining moment for Montana, marking its transition from a frontier territory to a full-fledged state within the Union. The establishment of a state government, the drafting of a constitution, and the challenges of managing diverse economic and social interests set the stage for Montana's future development. Statehood brought both opportunities and obstacles, as the people of Montana worked to build a society that balanced the promise of prosperity with the realities of frontier life.

As we move forward in Montana's history, we will see how the early foundations of governance, industry, and community laid during this period shaped the state's identity and trajectory. The challenges of balancing economic growth, political power, and the rights of all its citizens—including Native peoples, laborers, and settlers—would continue to be a theme that defined Montana's story in the years to come.

RANCHING & AGRICULTURE

As Montana moved into the late 19th and early 20th centuries, ranching and agriculture emerged as two of the key pillars of its economy, shaping both the landscape and the culture of the state. This chapter explores the rise of the cattle ranching industry, the development of homesteading, and the challenges faced by those who tried to make a living off the land in Montana's often harsh and unforgiving environment.

The Rise of Cattle Ranching

The cattle ranching industry in Montana began in earnest during the mid-1800s, driven by the increasing demand for beef across the United States. Vast stretches of open land, filled with native grasses and well-suited for grazing, made Montana an ideal location for large-scale cattle ranching. Cowboys and ranchers from Texas, Colorado, and other parts of the American West began driving herds north to

Montana, establishing the foundations of the state's cattle industry.

The completion of the Northern Pacific Railroad in the 1880s provided a critical link that allowed ranchers to transport cattle to markets across the country. With railroads facilitating the movement of livestock, Montana's cattle ranchers found a lucrative market for their beef, and cattle drives became a regular occurrence as herds were moved to railheads for shipment.

Large cattle companies, many of which were backed by investors from the East Coast or even overseas, began to acquire vast tracts of land, turning Montana into a hub of the cattle industry. The ranches that sprang up across the plains often stretched over thousands of acres, with herds numbering in the thousands. The open range, with no fences to limit movement, was seen as a land of opportunity, and cattle barons invested heavily in the growth of their herds.

Cowboys, who played a central role in the cattle industry, became symbols of Montana's frontier spirit. They lived a rugged, often dangerous life, working long hours to care for the herds, drive cattle across the plains, and protect them from rustlers and predators. The cowboy way of life became an enduring part of Montana's identity, celebrated in stories, songs, and folklore that captured the imagination of people far beyond the borders of the state.

However, the ranching boom of the 1880s was not without its challenges. By the late 1880s, the cattle industry was facing a crisis. The open range, once seen as limitless, began to show signs of overuse. Overstocking of cattle led to the depletion of native grasses, and overgrazing became a serious problem. The severe winter of 1886-1887, known as the "Big Die-Up," was a turning point for the cattle industry. Temperatures plummeted, and heavy snow blanketed the plains, leading to the death of thousands of cattle. Many ranchers were financially ruined, and the era of open-range ranching began to give way to a more regulated and controlled approach to cattle raising.

Homesteading and the Agricultural Boom

While ranching dominated Montana's economy in the early years, agriculture soon became an equally important force in the state's development. The Homestead Act of 1862 provided an incentive for settlers to move to Montana and other western territories, offering 160 acres of land to anyone willing to live on and improve it for at least five years. The act was intended to encourage the settlement of the western frontier, and Montana, with its wide-open spaces, became a prime destination for homesteaders.

The push for settlement gained momentum with the passage of the Enlarged Homestead Act of 1909, which increased the size of homesteads to 320 acres, making dryland farming more viable. This was followed by the

Stock-Raising Homestead Act of 1916, which offered 640-acre plots for grazing purposes. These acts spurred a wave of settlers into Montana, particularly during the early 20th century, as people from across the United States and even Europe moved to the state in search of land and opportunity.

Homesteaders faced significant challenges as they sought to carve out a living from the land. Montana's climate, with its harsh winters, hot summers, and unpredictable rainfall, made farming difficult. Many settlers arrived with dreams of prosperity, only to find that the reality of farming on the Great Plains was far more challenging than they had imagined. Crops such as wheat, barley, and oats were grown, but success depended heavily on the weather. Droughts, hailstorms, and pests could devastate a year's harvest, leaving homesteaders struggling to survive.

Despite these hardships, many homesteaders persevered, building communities and establishing the foundation for Montana's agricultural economy. Towns sprang up around farming areas, complete with schools, churches, and general stores. Cooperation among neighbors was essential, and the spirit of community helped settlers endure the difficult conditions they faced. Threshing bees, barn raisings, and community gatherings became important social events that provided a sense of camaraderie and mutual support.

Irrigation and Agricultural Innovation

The development of irrigation was a key factor in making agriculture more viable in Montana. The arid conditions of much of the state meant that successful farming often required a reliable water supply, and irrigation projects became a priority for both settlers and the state government. The Carey Land Act of 1894 allowed private companies to develop irrigation systems on federal land, and the Reclamation Act of 1902 further supported the construction of large-scale irrigation projects throughout the West.

The Sun River Project, initiated in the early 1900s, was one of Montana's earliest major irrigation projects, providing water to farms in the area surrounding Great Falls. Similar projects, such as the Milk River Project and the Huntley Project, were developed to bring water to dryland areas, transforming previously unproductive land into fertile farmland. Irrigation allowed farmers to grow more diverse crops and helped stabilize agricultural production, making Montana a significant producer of wheat and other grains.

Agricultural innovation also played a role in helping Montana's farmers adapt to the challenging environment. Dryland farming techniques, which emphasized moisture conservation and soil management, were developed to make the most of the limited rainfall. The use of drought-resistant crops, crop rotation, and new machinery all contributed to increased productivity, allowing farmers to overcome some of the obstacles posed by Montana's climate.

Boom and Bust in Agriculture

The early 20th century saw a period of prosperity for Montana's farmers, particularly during World War I, when the demand for wheat and other agricultural products soared. High prices and favorable conditions led to an agricultural boom, and many farmers took on debt to expand their operations, confident that the good times would continue. However, the boom was short-lived. After the war, prices for agricultural products plummeted, leaving many farmers unable to repay their loans.

The droughts of the 1920s and 1930s further compounded the challenges faced by Montana's farmers. The Dust Bowl, which affected much of the Great Plains, brought severe dust storms, crop failures, and economic hardship. Many farmers were forced to abandon their land, and rural communities that had once been thriving were left struggling to survive. The population of some farming areas declined as families moved elsewhere in search of better opportunities.

The federal government responded to the crisis with a series of New Deal programs aimed at providing relief to struggling farmers and stabilizing the agricultural economy. The Agricultural Adjustment Act, the Soil Conservation Service, and other programs offered financial assistance, promoted soil conservation practices, and helped farmers adopt new techniques to improve productivity. These efforts provided a measure of relief and laid the foundation for a more sustainable approach to agriculture in Montana.

The Legacy of Ranching and Agriculture

Ranching and agriculture have left an indelible mark on Montana's history, culture, and identity. The wide-open spaces, cattle drives, and the perseverance of homesteaders are all part of the state's enduring narrative. The challenges faced by ranchers and farmers—harsh winters, droughts, economic uncertainty—have fostered a culture of resilience and self-reliance that continues to define Montana's people.

Today, ranching and agriculture remain important parts of Montana's economy, though the industries have evolved significantly since their early days. Advances in technology, irrigation, and farming techniques have made agriculture more efficient and productive, while ranching continues to be a vital part of the state's rural communities. The legacy of the open range, the cowboy, and the homesteader lives on in the values and traditions of Montana's people, who continue to find ways to thrive in a land that is both beautiful and demanding.

As we move forward in Montana's history, we will see how the foundations laid by ranchers and homesteaders influenced the state's development in the 20th century and beyond. The story of Montana's agricultural and ranching communities is one of both hardship and triumph—a testament to the enduring connection between the land and the people who call it home.

INDUSTRIALIZATION & RESOURCE EXTRACTION

By the late 19th and early 20th centuries, Montana's economy was on the brink of a significant transformation. The discovery of rich mineral deposits, particularly copper, silver, and coal, coupled with an increasing demand for industrial resources, spurred the rapid industrialization of the state. Montana became a land of economic opportunity, attracting workers, entrepreneurs, and investors from across the nation and the world. However, the growth of resource extraction industries also brought environmental degradation, labor struggles, and conflicts over the control of wealth and power. In this chapter, we explore the rise of Montana's mining industry, the growth of railroads and infrastructure, and the complex impact of industrialization on the state's development.

The Mining Boom

Mining had always been a significant part of Montana's economy, beginning with the gold rushes of the 1860s. However, it was the discovery of copper that propelled Montana into the forefront of industrial resource extraction. In 1881, rich deposits of copper were discovered in Butte, which would soon earn the nickname "The Richest Hill on Earth." The demand for copper skyrocketed during this period, driven by the increasing use of electricity and the expansion of telegraph and telephone systems, which required vast amounts of copper wire.

The development of Butte's copper mines attracted significant investment, leading to the rapid growth of the mining industry. Marcus Daly, an Irish immigrant and one of the "Copper Kings" of Montana, played a central role in the development of the Anaconda Copper Mining Company, which would become one of the largest mining operations in the world. Daly, along with William A. Clark and F. Augustus Heinze, became prominent figures in Montana's mining industry, each vying for control of the lucrative copper market.

The mining boom transformed Butte from a small mining camp into a bustling industrial city, attracting thousands of workers from across the United States and abroad. Immigrants from countries like Ireland, Italy, Finland, and China flocked to Butte, seeking work in the mines and contributing to the city's diverse cultural landscape. Butte became a melting pot, with neighborhoods reflecting the ethnic backgrounds of its residents, and a thriving community life developed despite the harsh working conditions.

The Influence of the Copper Kings

The influence of the Copper Kings extended far beyond the mines of Butte. Marcus Daly, William Clark, and Augustus Heinze wielded immense economic and political power, shaping the development of Montana's infrastructure, politics, and society. Their rivalry, known as the "War of the Copper Kings," involved intense competition over control of mining claims, railroads, and even the state government.

William A. Clark, a wealthy entrepreneur and politician, used his fortune to build a political empire in Montana. He was instrumental in shaping the state's early political landscape, even serving as a U.S. Senator, although his tenure was marred by accusations of bribery and corruption. Clark's influence over Montana's political system led to widespread cynicism about the relationship between wealth and power, as he used his resources to influence elections and secure favorable policies.

Marcus Daly, on the other hand, focused much of his attention on building the Anaconda Copper Mining Company into a mining powerhouse. Daly established the town of Anaconda, which became the site of a massive copper smelter that processed ore from the Butte mines. Anaconda grew into an industrial hub, with the smelter employing thousands of workers and driving the local economy. Daly's investments in the Northern Pacific Railroad also helped expand transportation networks throughout the state, further facilitating the growth of industry.

The rivalry between the Copper Kings came to a head in a series of legal battles, political conflicts, and even physical confrontations over control of the copper industry. By the early 20th century, the Anaconda Copper Mining Company had emerged as the dominant force, consolidating its control over Montana's copper production and becoming one of the largest mining companies in the world. The company's influence over the state was so profound that it was often said Montana was "owned" by the Anaconda Company, a reflection of the immense power the corporation wielded over both the economy and politics.

Labor Struggles in the Mining Industry

The growth of the mining industry brought with it significant challenges, particularly for the men who worked in the mines. Working conditions in the mines were dangerous and grueling, with long hours, poor ventilation, and a constant risk of cave-ins, explosions, and accidents. Miners were often exposed to harmful dust and chemicals, which led to chronic health issues, including respiratory diseases like silicosis.

In response to these conditions, miners began to organize and form labor unions to fight for better wages, safer working conditions, and fair treatment. The Butte Miners' Union, established in 1878, was one of the earliest labor unions in Montana, and it quickly became a powerful force in advocating for workers' rights. The Western Federation of Miners (WFM), founded in 1893, played a central role in labor struggles across the American West, with Butte serving as one of its strongholds.

The labor movement in Montana was marked by strikes, protests, and conflicts between workers and mine owners. In 1914, the Anaconda Road Massacre occurred when miners on strike clashed with company guards, resulting in multiple deaths and injuries. The event highlighted the tensions between labor and capital in Montana's mining industry and underscored the lengths to which the mining companies would go to maintain control over their workers.

World War I brought new challenges to Montana's labor movement. The demand for copper increased dramatically, and the Anaconda Company ramped up production, placing even greater strain on workers. Labor unrest continued, culminating in the 1917 Speculator Mine disaster, the deadliest hard rock mining accident in U.S. history. A fire in the mine killed 168 men, sparking outrage among the mining community and leading to increased calls for safety reforms and better working conditions.

Environmental Impact of Mining

The rapid growth of mining and industrial activity in Montana had profound environmental consequences. The extraction of copper, silver, and other minerals left a lasting impact on the landscape, with open-pit mines, tailings piles, and smelter emissions contributing to widespread pollution. The town of Anaconda, home to the giant smelter, experienced significant environmental degradation due to the release of toxic chemicals, including arsenic and lead, which contaminated the soil, water, and air.

The Berkeley Pit, an open-pit copper mine in Butte, became a stark symbol of the environmental toll of mining. When the mine closed in 1982, the pit began to fill with water, creating a massive, toxic lake that remains one of the most polluted sites in the United States. The environmental legacy of mining in Montana has left communities grappling with health issues, economic decline, and the challenge of reclamation and cleanup efforts.

Despite the environmental costs, mining played a crucial role in Montana's economic development, providing jobs and generating wealth that supported the growth of cities and infrastructure. The prosperity brought by mining also facilitated the establishment of schools, hospitals, and public services that benefited the wider community. The challenge for Montana, however, has been to balance the economic benefits of resource extraction with the need to protect its natural environment for future generations.

Railroads and Infrastructure Development

The industrialization of Montana was closely linked to the expansion of its transportation infrastructure, particularly the railroads. The Northern Pacific Railroad, completed in the 1880s, was instrumental in connecting Montana's mines, farms, and ranches to markets across the country. Railroads facilitated the movement of minerals, cattle, and agricultural products, helping to integrate Montana's economy into the broader national economy.

The Great Northern Railway, established by James J. Hill, further expanded Montana's rail network, reaching towns and cities across the state and encouraging settlement and development. The arrival of the railroads brought new opportunities for economic growth, making it easier for settlers to move to Montana, for businesses to access supplies, and for farmers and ranchers to ship their products to distant markets.

The development of infrastructure also extended to urban areas, with cities like Butte, Helena, and Billings growing rapidly as centers of commerce, industry, and culture. Electric streetcars, paved roads, and public utilities became part of the urban landscape, transforming Montana's cities into bustling hubs of activity. The rise of industrial towns brought with it a new way of life, with theaters, saloons, social clubs, and labor halls all contributing to a vibrant community atmosphere.

Conclusion

The industrialization of Montana in the late 19th and early 20th centuries was a period of dramatic change, driven by the rapid growth of the mining industry and the expansion of railroads and infrastructure. The wealth generated by resource extraction brought prosperity and opportunity, attracting workers and investors from across the world and transforming Montana into an important center of industrial activity. However, this period was also marked by significant challenges—labor struggles, environmental degradation, and the concentration of economic and political power in the hands of a few.

The story of Montana's industrialization is a story of ambition, conflict, and resilience. The miners, railroad workers, and labor leaders who fought for fair treatment and better working conditions helped shape the state's identity, as did the entrepreneurs and investors who sought to harness its resources for profit. As we move forward in Montana's history, we will see how the legacy of industrialization, with its mix of triumphs and tribulations, continued to influence the state's development, shaping the communities, landscapes, and culture of this remarkable region.

THE CONSERVATION MOVEMENT

As Montana moved into the 20th century, the rapid industrialization of the state—driven by mining, logging, and agriculture—had a profound impact on its natural landscape. The unchecked extraction of resources led to widespread environmental degradation, prompting growing concern among residents and leaders about the future of Montana's wilderness and the sustainability of its natural resources. Out of this concern, a conservation movement began to take shape, one that would help define Montana's relationship with its environment and establish a balance between development and preservation.

This chapter explores the rise of the conservation movement in Montana, highlighting key figures, events, and efforts that sought to protect the state's natural beauty and ensure that its resources could be enjoyed by future generations. From the creation of Glacier National Park to the early wilderness protection efforts and the push for sustainable land use, this movement played a pivotal role in shaping Montana's identity as a state that values its natural heritage.

Early Conservation Efforts and National Parks

By the late 19th century, it was becoming clear that Montana's natural resources were not inexhaustible. The rapid growth of the mining industry, the expansion of logging operations, and the effects of overgrazing had taken a significant toll on the environment. Forests were being cut down at an alarming rate, rivers were polluted with tailings and chemicals from mining operations, and the once-abundant bison herds had been decimated.

The realization that these natural wonders could be lost spurred the beginnings of a conservation movement, led by individuals who saw the intrinsic value of Montana's landscapes. One of the most significant milestones in Montana's conservation history was the establishment of Glacier National Park in 1910. Located in the northern part of the state, Glacier National Park was created to preserve the spectacular mountainous region, which included pristine lakes, glaciers, and diverse wildlife. The park became a symbol of the conservation movement, highlighting the importance of protecting natural areas for public enjoyment and future generations.

The establishment of Glacier National Park was largely

due to the efforts of conservationists like George Bird Grinnell, who played a key role in lobbying for the park's creation. Grinnell, an anthropologist, writer, and early advocate for conservation, had spent years exploring the region and was deeply moved by its beauty. He recognized the need to protect it from exploitation and worked tirelessly to gain public support for its preservation. The park's designation was a major victory for the conservation movement, setting a precedent for future efforts to protect Montana's wilderness areas.

Yellowstone National Park, which straddled the border of Montana and Wyoming, also played a role in fostering a culture of conservation in the state. Established in 1872, Yellowstone was the first national park in the United States and the world, and its northern gateway was located in Gardiner, Montana. The park's creation was a landmark moment in the history of conservation, and it inspired efforts to preserve other unique landscapes across the American West.

Forest Conservation and the Birth of the U.S. Forest Service

The depletion of Montana's forests due to logging and other activities also became a focal point for conservation efforts. The early 20th century saw the rise of forestry as a profession, with leaders like Gifford Pinchot, the first chief of the U.S. Forest Service, advocating for the sustainable management of forest resources. Pinchot's philosophy of "wise use" emphasized the importance of balancing resource extraction with conservation, ensuring that forests could continue to provide timber, water, and recreational opportunities for future generations.

The establishment of the U.S. Forest Service in 1905 was a significant step toward protecting Montana's forests. The agency, which managed national forests and grasslands, worked to implement sustainable logging practices, prevent wildfires, and protect watersheds. The creation of national forests such as the Helena, Lolo, and Gallatin National Forests helped safeguard millions of acres of Montana's forestland, providing habitat for wildlife and recreational opportunities for the public.

One of the most influential figures in Montana's forest conservation movement was Elers Koch, a forester who worked for the U.S. Forest Service in the early 1900s. Koch was instrumental in developing fire suppression strategies and implementing sustainable logging practices in Montana's forests. He recognized the importance of maintaining healthy ecosystems and worked to ensure that logging was conducted in a way that minimized environmental impact. His efforts helped lay the foundation for modern forestry practices in the state and contributed to the broader conservation movement.

The Role of Wilderness Advocacy

As Montana's population grew and more land was developed for agriculture, mining, and ranching, the desire to protect wild and undeveloped areas gained momentum. The wilderness advocacy movement emerged in response to concerns that Montana's natural landscapes were being lost to human activity, and it aimed to preserve these areas in their natural state, free from roads, logging, and other forms of development.

One of the early leaders of the wilderness movement in Montana was Bob Marshall, a forester, writer, and co-founder of the Wilderness Society. Marshall, who spent much of his life exploring Montana's mountains and forests, was a passionate advocate for wilderness preservation. He believed that wilderness areas provided not only a refuge for wildlife but also a place where people could connect with nature and experience solitude. His writings and advocacy helped inspire the passage of the Wilderness Act of 1964, which established a system for designating and protecting wilderness areas across the United States.

In Montana, the passage of the Wilderness Act led to the designation of several wilderness areas, including the Bob Marshall Wilderness, named in honor of Bob Marshall's contributions to the movement. The Bob Marshall Wilderness, established in 1964, is one of the largest wilderness areas in the contiguous United States, encompassing over a million acres of pristine forests, rivers, and mountains. It remains a testament to the dedication of conservationists who worked to ensure that Montana's wild places would be preserved for future generations.

The Conservation Legacy of the Anaconda Company

The influence of the Anaconda Copper Mining Company on Montana's economy and environment cannot be overstated. While the company played a significant role in the state's industrial development, it also left behind a legacy of environmental degradation, particularly in the form of pollution from smelters and mining operations. By the mid-20th century, concerns about the environmental impact of the Anaconda Company's activities were growing, and the company began to take steps to address these issues.

In the 1950s and 1960s, the Anaconda Company initiated efforts to mitigate the environmental damage caused by its operations. This included reforestation projects, soil stabilization, and measures to reduce air pollution from its smelters. These efforts, while limited in scope, represented an early recognition of the need for environmental responsibility in the resource extraction industry. The company's actions also highlighted the growing awareness of environmental issues among the public and the need for greater oversight and regulation of industrial activities.

The decline of the Anaconda Company in the 1970s and 1980s led to increased attention on the environmental cleanup of mining sites. The Berkeley Pit in Butte, one of the most notorious examples of environmental damage from mining, became a focal point for reclamation efforts. In 1983, the Environmental Protection Agency (EPA) designated the area as a Superfund site, initiating a long-term effort to clean up the contaminated water and soil. The reclamation of mining sites across Montana remains an ongoing challenge, but it also reflects the growing commitment to addressing the environmental legacy of resource extraction.

Modern Conservation Efforts and Public Lands

In the latter half of the 20th century, conservation efforts in Montana expanded beyond wilderness preservation to include broader issues such as wildlife management, water quality, and public access to natural areas. The establishment of state parks, wildlife refuges, and conservation easements helped protect important habitats and ensure that Montana's natural resources were managed sustainably.

One of the key successes of the modern conservation movement has been the preservation of public lands for recreational use. The public lands debate in Montana has been a central issue, with conservationists advocating for the protection of these lands from privatization and development. The state's national forests, parks, and wilderness areas provide opportunities for hiking, fishing, hunting, and other outdoor activities, contributing to

Montana's reputation as a destination for outdoor enthusiasts and helping support the state's growing tourism industry.

Conservation organizations such as the Montana Wilderness Association, the Greater Yellowstone Coalition, and the Nature Conservancy have played a significant role in advocating for the protection of Montana's natural areas. These organizations work to build public support for conservation initiatives, lobby for protective legislation, and collaborate with landowners, businesses, and government agencies to promote sustainable land use practices.

The reintroduction of species such as the gray wolf into Yellowstone National Park has also been a notable success for conservation in Montana. The reintroduction, which began in 1995, has helped restore ecological balance to the region, demonstrating the importance of protecting entire ecosystems rather than focusing solely on individual species. The presence of wolves has had a positive impact on the health of the park's ecosystem, leading to increased biodiversity and the recovery of species that depend on a balanced food chain.

The conservation movement in Montana has been shaped by the state's unique natural beauty and the recognition that its resources are both valuable and vulnerable. From the creation of Glacier National Park to the establishment of wilderness areas, national forests, and public lands, the movement has sought to balance the needs of development with the imperative to protect Montana's environment for future generations.

The legacy of conservation in Montana is one of resilience, advocacy, and a deep connection to the land. The efforts of early conservationists like George Bird Grinnell, Bob Marshall, and others have left a lasting impact on the state, ensuring that Montana's wild places continue to thrive and inspire. Today, Montana's conservation movement continues to evolve, facing new challenges such as climate change, population growth, and the pressures of modern development. As we move forward, the lessons of the past remind us of the importance of preserving the natural heritage that makes Montana such a special place, both for those who call it home and for those who come to experience its beauty.

THE GREAT DERESSION & WWII

The 20th century brought with it economic highs and lows for Montana, defined most notably by the impacts of the Great Depression and World War II. The economic boom of the early 20th century, driven by mining, agriculture, and industry, gave way to hardship during the Depression, while World War II brought new opportunities, economic growth, and significant changes in society. This chapter explores Montana's experience during these pivotal decades, highlighting the challenges of the Great Depression, the role of the New Deal, and the state's contributions during World War II.

The Boom Before the Bust

Montana entered the 1920s on the heels of an agricultural boom driven by high demand for wheat and other crops during World War I. Farmers expanded their operations, taking on debt to buy new equipment and land, confident that high prices would continue indefinitely. Mining, ranching, and railroads also thrived, buoyed by the state's abundant natural resources and growing infrastructure.

However, by the late 1920s, Montana's prosperity began to unravel. Overproduction in agriculture led to a drop in crop prices, and many farmers, burdened by debt, found themselves unable to make ends meet. The state's mining sector, which had long been a cornerstone of its economy, also faced challenges as copper prices fell due to declining demand. As these industries faltered, the state's economy became increasingly vulnerable.

The Onset of the Great Depression

When the stock market crashed in 1929, it sent shockwaves through Montana's already struggling economy. The collapse of commodity prices devastated farmers, and many lost their land to foreclosure. Banks that had extended loans to farmers and businesses began to fail, and the resulting wave of bankruptcies and unemployment affected communities across the state. The impact was particularly severe in rural areas, where entire families were forced off their land, leaving behind abandoned farms and empty towns.

The mining industry, too, suffered greatly during the Great Depression. The Anaconda Copper Mining Company, one of the largest employers in the state, cut production, laid off workers, and closed several mines. Towns like Butte, which had thrived during the copper boom, experienced a sharp decline, with unemployment reaching alarming levels. The economic hardship of the Great Depression left many Montanans without jobs, income, or hope for the future.

The Great Depression also had a significant impact on the cultural and social fabric of Montana. Families who had once been self-sufficient found themselves relying on charity and government assistance to get by. Many people left the state in search of better opportunities elsewhere, contributing to a decline in Montana's population during the 1930s. Those who remained often banded together, relying on neighbors and community networks to survive the difficult times.

The New Deal in Montana

In response to the widespread economic hardship, President Franklin D. Roosevelt's New Deal programs sought to provide relief, recovery, and reform to the nation, and Montana was no exception. The New Deal brought a wave of federal assistance to the state, providing much-needed jobs and infrastructure improvements that helped alleviate the worst effects of the Depression.

The Civilian Conservation Corps (CCC) was one of the most popular New Deal programs in Montana. The CCC provided jobs for young men, who worked on projects such as reforestation, soil conservation, and the construction of parks and trails. In Montana, CCC crews built campgrounds, fire lookout towers, and trails in places like Glacier National Park, improving access to the state's natural areas while providing employment and training for thousands of young men.

The Works Progress Administration (WPA) was another key New Deal program that made a significant impact in Montana. The WPA funded a wide variety of projects, from building schools, bridges, and roads to supporting artists, writers, and musicians. In Montana, WPA workers constructed public buildings, improved infrastructure, and created murals and public art that celebrated the state's history and culture. The projects provided jobs for unemployed workers and left a lasting legacy in the form of infrastructure and cultural enrichment.

The Agricultural Adjustment Administration (AAA) sought to stabilize crop prices by reducing agricultural overproduction. In Montana, the AAA paid farmers to reduce their wheat acreage, which helped to alleviate the glut of wheat on the market. While the program provided some relief to struggling farmers, it also had the unintended consequence of forcing many small farmers off their land, as larger landowners consolidated their holdings to take advantage of government payments.

The New Deal's impact on Montana was transformative, providing not only economic relief but also a sense of hope and possibility for the future. While the state continued to face significant challenges throughout the 1930s, the federal programs helped to lay the foundation for economic recovery and provided a safety net for those who had been hit hardest by the Depression.

World War II and Economic Recovery

The outbreak of World War II in 1939, and the United States' entry into the conflict in 1941, marked the beginning of a new chapter for Montana. The war effort brought a surge in demand for natural resources, labor, and production, leading to an economic boom that helped pull Montana out of the Great Depression.

Montana's mining industry, which had languished during the 1930s, experienced a revival as the demand for copper, zinc, manganese, and other minerals surged. The Anaconda Copper Mining Company ramped up production to support the war effort, and the mines of Butte once again became a critical source of copper, which was used in everything from electrical wiring to ammunition. The increased production brought jobs and prosperity back to mining towns, revitalizing local economies that had struggled during the Depression.

In addition to mining, Montana's agricultural sector played an important role in the war effort. Farmers increased their production of wheat, livestock, and other essential commodities to feed both the military and the civilian population. The federal government encouraged farmers to maximize output, and wartime demand led to higher prices, providing a much-needed boost to Montana's agricultural economy. Many farmers who had struggled through the 1930s finally found themselves on more stable financial ground.

Montana also contributed to the war effort through the establishment of military installations and training facilities. Malmstrom Air Force Base, originally known as the Great Falls Army Air Base, was constructed in 1942 and became an important training site for bomber crews during the war. The presence of military bases brought new jobs and economic activity to Montana, as well as a sense of pride in the state's contribution to the national defense.

The people of Montana played a significant role in supporting the war effort, both at home and abroad. Thousands of Montanans enlisted in the armed forces, serving in every branch of the military and in theaters of war around the world. On the home front, women entered the workforce in greater numbers, taking jobs in factories, mines, and other industries to replace the men who had gone off to fight. The war brought significant social changes to Montana, challenging traditional gender roles and laying the groundwork for future shifts in the workforce.

Post-War Changes and Challenges

The end of World War II in 1945 brought both opportunities and challenges for Montana. The wartime economic boom began to taper off as demand for minerals and agricultural products declined, and the state faced the task of transitioning to a peacetime economy. Many veterans returned home, seeking jobs, education, and a sense of normalcy after the disruptions of war. The G.I. Bill provided educational and housing benefits to returning servicemen, and many veterans took advantage of these opportunities to attend college or purchase land.

In agriculture, the post-war period saw the introduction of new technologies and mechanization that transformed farming practices. Tractors, combines, and other machinery made farming more efficient, but also led to the consolidation of small farms into larger operations. Many small farmers found it difficult to compete with the larger, mechanized farms and were forced to sell their land. This trend contributed to the decline of rural communities across the state, as young people left farming areas in search of better opportunities in cities.

The mining industry also faced changes in the post-war period. While copper production remained important, the industry began to shift toward other minerals, such as coal and uranium. The rise of strip mining and open-pit mining techniques brought new environmental challenges, as the impacts of resource extraction became more visible on the landscape. The legacy of environmental degradation from mining would become an increasingly important issue for Montana in the years to come, as residents sought to balance economic growth with the need to protect the state's natural resources.

The Great Depression and World War II were transformative periods for Montana, reshaping the state's economy, society, and culture. The hardships of the Depression tested the resilience of Montana's people, but the New Deal provided a lifeline that helped many families survive and set the stage for future growth. World War II brought economic recovery, new opportunities, and significant social change, as Montanans contributed to the war effort both at home and on the front lines.

The post-war period brought its own challenges, as Montana sought to navigate the transition from a wartime to a peacetime economy. The rise of mechanization and the consolidation of industries changed the face of agriculture and mining, while the environmental impacts of resource extraction became a growing concern. As Montana moved into the latter half of the 20th century, the state faced new questions about how to balance economic growth with the need to protect its land, people, and way of life.

The resilience and adaptability shown by Montanans during these decades laid the foundation for the future, as the state continued to evolve in response to changing economic, social, and environmental conditions. The lessons learned during the Great Depression and World War II would continue to shape Montana's identity, reminding its people of the importance of community, perseverance, and the enduring connection to the land.

POST-WAR GROWTH & MODERNIZATION

After World War II, Montana experienced a period of transformation as the state adapted to post-war growth and modernization. The economic boom of the post-war years brought new opportunities and challenges, as Montana's economy shifted from one dominated by agriculture and mining to one that included new industries such as tourism, technology, and energy production. The social and cultural landscape of Montana also changed during this period, as new infrastructure, urbanization, and evolving demographics redefined the state's identity.

This chapter explores the post-war decades in Montana, highlighting the economic, social, and political changes that shaped the state during the latter half of the 20th century. From the rise of tourism and the development of new infrastructure to the challenges posed by environmental concerns and the push for greater political representation, these years were a time of significant change for Montana and its people.

Economic Diversification and Challenges

Montana entered the post-war period with a strong sense of optimism, buoyed by the economic boom that followed World War II. The agricultural sector benefited from improved technology and mechanization, which made farming more efficient and productive. New machinery, fertilizers, and pesticides helped increase crop yields, and many farmers embraced these innovations. However, the increased costs associated with mechanization also contributed to the consolidation of farms, with smaller, family-owned operations often unable to compete with larger, more industrialized farms.

Mining remained a significant part of Montana's economy, but the industry faced challenges as it adapted to changing market conditions. Copper production continued, but the rise of open-pit mining brought new environmental and social consequences. The Berkeley Pit in Butte, one of the largest open-pit mines in the world, became emblematic of the environmental toll of resource extraction. The closure of underground mines in Butte in the 1950s and 1960s marked the beginning of a shift in the mining industry, as open-pit operations took center stage. This change resulted in significant job losses, and many mining communities struggled to adapt to the new reality.

The post-war years also saw the growth of the coal industry in Montana. The rich coal deposits of eastern Montana attracted interest from energy companies, and by the 1970s, coal mining had become a major industry in the state. The construction of coal-fired power plants and the development of strip mining operations brought new economic opportunities, but also sparked debates about the environmental impacts of coal extraction and combustion.

The Rise of Tourism

As Montana's traditional industries faced economic ups and downs, tourism emerged as an important and growing sector of the state's economy. Montana's stunning natural beauty, with its mountains, lakes, rivers, and national parks, attracted visitors from across the country and around the world. The completion of new highways and the growth of the automobile industry made it easier for tourists to travel to Montana, and tourism became a significant contributor to the state's economy.

Glacier and Yellowstone National Parks became major attractions, drawing visitors interested in experiencing the wilderness and wildlife of Montana. The rise of outdoor recreation activities such as hiking, camping, fishing, and hunting helped fuel the growth of tourism, and small towns near the parks, such as West Yellowstone and Whitefish, saw their economies transformed by the influx of visitors. The tourism industry provided jobs in hospitality, retail, and services, helping diversify Montana's economy and providing new opportunities for local communities.

The rise of tourism also led to increased awareness of the need to protect Montana's natural resources. Conservation efforts gained momentum as more people recognized the importance of preserving the state's natural beauty, both for its intrinsic value and for its economic benefits. The tourism industry became a powerful advocate for environmental protection, supporting initiatives to maintain clean rivers, healthy forests, and abundant wildlife populations.

Infrastructure and Urbanization

The post-war period brought significant investments in infrastructure that helped modernize Montana's cities and rural communities. The construction of highways, schools, hospitals, and public utilities transformed the state, improving the quality of life for its residents and laying the foundation for future growth.

The Federal-Aid Highway Act of 1956, which funded the construction of the Interstate Highway System, had a major impact on Montana. The construction of Interstate 90 (I-90) and Interstate 15 (I-15) connected Montana's cities to the rest of the country, making travel and commerce easier and more efficient. Improved transportation networks facilitated the movement of goods, people, and services, helping boost economic activity and encouraging the growth of cities like

Billings, Missoula, and Great Falls.

Urbanization also became a defining feature of Montana's post-war growth. While agriculture and mining continued to play important roles in the state's economy, more Montanans moved to urban areas in search of jobs, education, and better living conditions. The growth of cities brought new amenities, such as shopping centers, cultural institutions, and entertainment venues, which contributed to a more diverse and vibrant urban culture.

The post-war baby boom also played a role in shaping Montana's demographics. The population increased as families grew, and new suburban neighborhoods sprang up around cities. The demand for education led to the expansion of the state's university system, with institutions like the University of Montana in Missoula and Montana State University in Bozeman growing in size and influence. These universities became centers of education, research, and cultural life, contributing to the modernization of Montana and helping shape the state's future leaders.

Environmental Concerns and Activism

As Montana modernized and its economy diversified, concerns about the environmental impacts of industrial activity began to gain traction. The environmental movement of the 1960s and 1970s, which swept across the United States, found a strong foothold in Montana. The state's natural beauty and the visible impacts of mining, logging, and coal extraction inspired many Montanans to become advocates for environmental protection.

One of the most significant environmental issues in Montana during this period was the impact of the Berkeley Pit in Butte. The open-pit mine, which operated from 1955 to 1982, became a symbol of the environmental costs of mining. When the mine closed, the pit began to fill with highly acidic water, contaminated with heavy metals and other pollutants. The Berkeley Pit became one of the largest Superfund sites in the United States, highlighting the long-term environmental consequences of resource extraction.

The push for environmental protection led to the passage of new regulations aimed at reducing pollution and protecting Montana's natural resources. The Montana Environmental Policy Act (MEPA), passed in 1971, was one of the first state-level environmental policy acts in the nation. Modeled after the National Environmental Policy Act (NEPA), MEPA required state agencies to assess the environmental impacts of their actions and involve the public in decision-making processes.

The fight over coal mining and energy development in eastern Montana also became a major issue during this period. The proposed development of coal mines and power plants in the Powder River Basin sparked debates about the environmental impacts of strip mining, air and water pollution, and the long-term sustainability of energy production. Grassroots organizations, environmental groups, and concerned citizens rallied to protect Montana's landscapes, leading to a series of legal battles and public protests that helped shape state policy.

One of the most notable victories for Montana's environmental movement was the passage of the Montana Coal Severance Tax in 1975. The tax, which imposed a fee on coal extraction, was used to fund public programs, infrastructure projects, and environmental cleanup efforts. The tax helped ensure that the benefits of resource extraction were shared with the broader community, while also providing funds to address the environmental impacts of mining.

Political Changes and Shifts

The post-war period also brought political changes to Montana, as the state's demographics, economy, and society evolved. The rise of the environmental movement, the diversification of the economy, and the growth of urban areas contributed to shifts in political power and priorities.

Montana's political landscape was marked by a mix of conservatism and progressivism, reflecting the diverse interests of the state's residents. The agricultural and ranching communities in rural areas tended to favor conservative policies, while the urban areas and university towns leaned toward more progressive views. The state's history of labor activism, rooted in the mining industry, also contributed to a tradition of political engagement and advocacy for workers' rights.

In 1972, Montana adopted a new state constitution, which was seen as one of the most progressive in the nation at the time. The new constitution included provisions for environmental protection, public participation in government, and the right to privacy and individual dignity. The constitutional convention that drafted the document was notable for its inclusiveness, with a diverse group of delegates working to create a framework that reflected the values and aspirations of modern Montana.

The new constitution also established a more transparent and accountable government, with measures aimed at reducing the influence of corporate interests and ensuring that public officials were responsive to the needs of the people. The adoption of the 1972 constitution marked a turning point in Montana's political history, as the state sought to redefine itself in a rapidly changing world.

Cultural Shifts and Modern Montana

The post-war decades also brought cultural changes to Montana, as new influences and ideas reshaped the state's identity. The rise of television, the growth of the university system, and the increased mobility of the population brought

Montanans into closer contact with national and global trends. The counterculture movement of the 1960s and 1970s found expression in Montana, particularly in university towns like Missoula, where students and activists embraced new ideas about civil rights, environmentalism, and social justice.

The growth of tourism also contributed to cultural shifts, as visitors from across the country and around the world brought new perspectives to Montana. The state's natural beauty, outdoor recreational opportunities, and Western heritage attracted people who were drawn to the idea of the "last best place"—a phrase that came to symbolize Montana's unique blend of rugged individualism, natural splendor, and a slower pace of life.

The latter half of the 20th century also saw a renewed focus on the rights and cultural heritage of Native American tribes in Montana. The civil rights movement of the 1960s and 1970s inspired Native American activists to push for greater recognition of their rights, sovereignty, and cultural traditions. Tribal colleges were established to provide educational opportunities for Native students, and efforts were made to preserve Native languages, traditions, and cultural practices. The relationship between the state government and Montana's Native tribes evolved during this period, with increased recognition of tribal sovereignty and the importance of honoring treaty obligations.

A BRIEF HISTORY OF MONTANA

The decades following World War II were a time of significant growth, change, and modernization for Montana. The state's economy diversified, with tourism, energy production, and technology joining agriculture and mining as key industries. The rise of environmental concerns and the push for conservation reflected a growing awareness of the need to balance economic development with the protection of Montana's natural resources.

Montana's post-war history is a story of adaptation and resilience, as the state's residents navigated the challenges of modernization while striving to maintain the values that defined their way of life. The shifts in politics, culture, and society that took place during these years laid the foundation for the Montana of today—a state that values its natural beauty, embraces its cultural diversity, and continues to balance the demands of progress with the need to protect its unique heritage.

As we move into the 21st century, the lessons of the past remain relevant, reminding us of the importance of community, stewardship, and the enduring connection between Montana's people and the land they call home.

CONTEMPORARY ERA

The dawn of the 21st century brought with it a host of new opportunities and challenges for Montana. The state, known for its rugged beauty, rich natural resources, and storied history, found itself navigating the complexities of a modern world while trying to preserve its distinct identity and heritage. Montana's contemporary era has been marked by a blend of growth, cultural shifts, and a renewed focus on sustainability, all within the context of a rapidly evolving social and economic landscape.

This chapter explores the key developments that have shaped Montana from the 2000s onward, including economic diversification, demographic changes, the rise of technology, and the growing emphasis on conservation and environmental stewardship. Montana's journey into the 21st century has been characterized by a delicate balance between growth and preservation, between new opportunities and old challenges.

Economic Diversification and Growth

As the 21st century began, Montana continued to diversify its economy beyond the traditional industries of agriculture and mining. While these industries remained vital to the state's identity and economy, new sectors such as technology, tourism, and renewable energy began to play increasingly significant roles. The diversification of Montana's economy was key to its growth and resilience, allowing the state to adapt to changing market conditions and global trends.

The technology sector, in particular, experienced notable growth during the early 2000s. Bozeman, home to Montana State University, emerged as a hub for tech startups and innovation. The university's strong engineering and computer science programs helped fuel the growth of a vibrant tech community, attracting entrepreneurs and investors interested in tapping into Montana's talent pool and quality of life. Companies specializing in software development, biotechnology, and data analytics found a welcoming environment in Montana, contributing to the state's economic diversification and creating new job opportunities.

Tourism also continued to be a significant driver of Montana's economy. The state's national parks, including Glacier and Yellowstone, remained major attractions, drawing millions of visitors each year. Outdoor recreation, such as skiing, fly fishing, hiking, and hunting, became increasingly popular, helping to support local businesses and communities. Tourism provided a steady source of revenue for the state, helping to offset downturns in other sectors and boosting the economy of many small towns.

Renewable energy development became a focal point for Montana in the 21st century. With its vast open spaces and abundant natural resources, Montana was well-positioned to capitalize on wind, solar, and hydroelectric power. Wind farms sprang up in eastern Montana, taking advantage of the region's steady winds to generate clean energy. The state also invested in solar projects and hydroelectric power generation, aiming to diversify its energy portfolio and reduce its reliance on fossil fuels.

Demographic Changes and Urban Growth

The early 21st century saw significant demographic changes in Montana. As technology and tourism flourished, more people were drawn to the state's quality of life, including its open spaces, access to outdoor recreation, and relatively low cost of living. Cities like Bozeman, Missoula, and Billings experienced population growth, attracting young professionals, retirees, and families seeking a slower pace of life. Bozeman, in particular, became one of the fastest-growing cities in the country, with an influx of newcomers drawn by the tech industry and the proximity to

Yellowstone National Park.

The population growth brought both opportunities and challenges. On the one hand, the influx of new residents provided a boost to local economies, supported the growth of businesses, and increased the tax base. On the other hand, the rapid growth put pressure on infrastructure, housing, and public services. Housing affordability became a major issue, particularly in cities like Bozeman and Missoula, where rising demand drove up property prices and rental costs. The challenge of balancing growth with maintaining the character of these communities became a key issue for local leaders.

Rural Montana, meanwhile, continued to face challenges related to population decline and limited economic opportunities. Many rural communities struggled to retain young people, who often left in search of education and employment elsewhere. The decline of small-scale agriculture, combined with the mechanization of farming, led to fewer jobs in rural areas. However, some rural communities found ways to adapt, embracing tourism, renewable energy development, and niche agriculture as ways to revitalize their economies.

Native American Communities and Cultural Revitalization

Montana is home to twelve federally recognized Native American tribes, each with its own history, culture, and traditions. The 21st century has seen a renewed focus on the rights and cultural revitalization of Native American communities in Montana. Tribal sovereignty, economic development, and the preservation of cultural heritage have been central issues for the state's Native population, as tribes work to assert their rights and strengthen their communities.

Economic development initiatives on Montana's reservations have focused on creating sustainable opportunities that respect tribal culture and sovereignty. Tribes have pursued a range of initiatives, from renewable energy projects and tourism to agriculture and entrepreneurship. The Blackfeet Nation, for example, has invested in wind energy, while the Fort Peck Assiniboine and Sioux Tribes have developed buffalo herds as part of their efforts to restore traditional practices and promote food sovereignty.

Education and cultural preservation have also been key areas of focus. Tribal colleges, such as Salish Kootenai College and Chief Dull Knife College, play an important role in providing educational opportunities for Native students, while also serving as centers for cultural preservation and community development. Efforts to revitalize Native languages have gained momentum, with language immersion programs, cultural camps, and partnerships with universities helping to ensure that these languages are passed on to future generations.

Environmental Stewardship and Conservation

Montana's natural beauty has always been one of its defining features, and the importance of protecting the environment has only grown in the 21st century. The state has faced a range of environmental challenges, including climate change, the impacts of resource extraction, and the need to balance economic growth with conservation.

The effects of climate change have been particularly evident in Montana, where rising temperatures, prolonged droughts, and changing precipitation patterns have impacted agriculture, wildlife, and water resources. Glacier National Park, one of Montana's most iconic natural areas, has seen its glaciers shrink dramatically in recent decades, serving as a visible reminder of the impact of a warming climate. The challenge of adapting to these changes while mitigating future impacts has become a central focus for policymakers, scientists, and conservationists.

Montana's agricultural sector has also had to adapt to the realities of climate change. Drought-resistant crops, improved irrigation techniques, and sustainable farming practices have become increasingly important as farmers work to maintain productivity in the face of changing conditions. The rise of regenerative agriculture, which focuses on soil health and carbon sequestration, has provided a path forward for some farmers looking to reduce their environmental impact and improve the resilience of their operations.

Conservation organizations have played a key role in protecting Montana's landscapes and wildlife. Groups like the Montana Wilderness Association, Trout Unlimited, and the Greater Yellowstone Coalition have worked to preserve public lands, restore native fish populations, and advocate for sustainable land management practices. Public lands have remained a contentious issue in Montana, with debates over their use, management, and ownership continuing to shape state politics. However, a broad coalition of stakeholders—including conservationists, hunters, anglers, and outdoor enthusiasts—has come together to support the protection of these lands for future generations.

Political Dynamics and Social Change

Montana's political landscape in the 21st century has been characterized by a mix of conservatism and progressivism, reflecting the diverse interests of the state's population. Rural areas have tended to lean conservative, with a focus on issues such as property rights, limited government, and the Second Amendment, while urban areas and university towns have been more progressive, advocating for environmental protection, education, and social justice.

The political divisions in Montana have been evident in statewide elections, which have often been closely contested. The state has elected both Republican and Democratic governors, senators, and representatives, reflecting its status as a battleground state. Issues such as healthcare, public land access, and economic development have been central to political debates, as Montanans seek to balance the values of independence and self-reliance with the need for government support and services.

Social change has also been a significant theme in contemporary Montana. The state has seen growing diversity, with new residents bringing different perspectives and cultures to Montana's communities. The LGBTQ+ community has gained visibility and acceptance, with advocacy groups working to ensure equal rights and protections for all Montanans. The Black Lives Matter movement and other social justice initiatives have sparked conversations about race, equity, and inclusion, prompting reflection on Montana's history and its future.

The Covid-19 Pandemic and Its Impact

The Covid-19 pandemic, which began in early 2020, had a profound impact on Montana, as it did on the rest of the world. The pandemic brought significant challenges, including public health crises, economic disruptions, and social isolation. Hospitals, particularly in rural areas, faced strain as they worked to treat patients, and the state implemented public health measures to slow the spread of the virus.

The economic impact of the pandemic was felt across many sectors, particularly tourism, hospitality, and small businesses. However, Montana's outdoor recreation industry experienced a surge in interest, as people sought opportunities to escape crowded urban areas and enjoy nature in a socially distanced manner. The pandemic underscored the importance of outdoor spaces for physical and mental well-being, reinforcing Montana's status as a destination for outdoor enthusiasts.

The pandemic also accelerated changes in the way people lived and worked. Remote work became more common, and many people chose to relocate to Montana, drawn by its quality of life and access to the outdoors. The influx of new residents brought both opportunities and challenges, as communities worked to accommodate growth while maintaining the character and values that made Montana an attractive place to live.

Montana's journey through the contemporary era has been one of growth, adaptation, and resilience. The state has faced the challenges of a changing economy, shifting demographics, and evolving social and environmental issues, all while striving to maintain its unique identity and connection to the land. The balance between growth and preservation, between opportunity and challenge, has defined Montana's experience in the 21st century.

As Montana continues to evolve, the lessons of the past

remain relevant. The values of independence, community, and stewardship that have shaped Montana's history continue to guide its people as they navigate the complexities of a modern world. The challenges of climate change, economic development, and social inclusion will require creative solutions, collaboration, and a commitment to the values that make Montana a special place.

The story of Montana is one of perseverance, adaptation, and a deep connection to the land and its people. As we look to the future, the spirit of Montana—shaped by its landscapes, its history, and its people—remains as strong and enduring as ever.

CONCLUSION

Montana's story is one of resilience, transformation, and a deep and abiding connection to the land. From the time of the first Indigenous peoples who lived in harmony with the plains, mountains, and rivers, through the waves of exploration, settlement, and development, the history of Montana is one of adaptation to both opportunities and challenges. The journey of Montana has been defined by its stunning landscapes, natural resources, diverse cultures, and a spirit of independence that remains as strong today as ever.

Throughout the centuries, Montana has been shaped by the forces of exploration, mining, ranching, agriculture, conservation, and industry. Each era brought new changes—some promising and others fraught with hardship. The gold rush and the boom-and-bust cycles of mining left their mark not only on the economy but also on the spirit of the people. The rise of agriculture and ranching molded communities that thrived on hard work, cooperation, and the promise of a better life. The conservation movement, a response to the excesses of unchecked resource extraction, embodied Montana's commitment to preserving its natural wonders for future generations.

The Great Depression tested the resolve of Montana's people, but it also brought about new approaches to governance, community, and economic resilience. The New Deal helped lay the groundwork for recovery, while World War II and the post-war years brought growth, modernization, and a new understanding of Montana's place in the wider world. As the economy diversified in the 20th century, Montana embraced tourism, technology, and renewable energy, all while continuing to honor its agricultural and mining heritage.

Today, Montana stands at the crossroads of tradition and innovation. It is a place where the cowboy and the coder coexist, where the majesty of the wilderness draws millions of visitors, and where communities work to balance progress with preservation. The issues facing Montana in the contemporary era—economic inequality, climate change, environmental stewardship, and cultural inclusion—are complex, but they are being addressed with the same determination that has defined the state for generations.

Montana's future will be shaped by its people: the farmers, ranchers, teachers, workers, artists, and leaders who call it home. The state's identity is woven from many threads—the legacies of its Native tribes, the spirit of the pioneers, the resilience of miners and laborers, and the conservation ethos of those who seek to protect its natural heritage. Each of these stories is part of a larger tapestry that continues to evolve, reflecting the beauty, challenges, and opportunities that make Montana unique.

As we look forward, Montana's past offers valuable lessons: the importance of community, the need to care for the land, and the strength that comes from facing adversity with determination. By honoring the past while embracing new possibilities, Montana can continue to thrive, ensuring that its natural beauty, rich culture, and indomitable spirit endure for generations to come.

Montana remains, as it always has been, a place where the vastness of the landscape mirrors the potential of its people—a place of untamed beauty, deep roots, and an enduring promise.

ABOUT THE AUTHOR

KJ Smith is an amateur historian with a passion for uncovering the stories that have shaped America's diverse states and regions. A lifelong learner and avid traveler, KJ has spent years exploring the landscapes, landmarks, and local histories that bring each state's unique character to life.

With an approachable writing style and a deep curiosity for the past, KJ aims to make history accessible and engaging for readers of all backgrounds. Whether diving into the founding of a state, its cultural milestones, or its unsung heroes, KJ brings a fresh perspective and genuine enthusiasm to every page.

When not researching or writing, KJ enjoys visiting historical sites, hiking scenic trails, and connecting with communities to hear their stories firsthand. *A Brief History* series is KJ's tribute to the rich and varied tapestry of American history—one state at a time.

Printed in Dunstable, United Kingdom